YOU WRITE THE SONGS

Welcome to "You Write the Songs," a great new tool to help lyricists complete the journey to "songwriter." We are providing you with a series of musical "templates," created by top Nashville studio musicians. Each template is a complete song, written in the styles and tempos that are appropriate for a specific genre of music. Along with the music soundtrack, you will also find a "chord chart" that will lead you through the sections of the template, to make it clear as we progress from section to section. The intros, verses, choruses, bridges, and instrumental sections will be clearly marked, and obvious in the recording as well. Your job will be to listen to the music, close your eyes, and let the "songwriter" in you go to work. Like many writers, you probably have notebooks full of lyrics. Listen to this music, and try to find a good fit. And because of the copyright laws in the U.S. and around the world, when you finish creating your melody and lyrics, and applying them to our template, you have written a "song." You may feel free to copyright and/or publish these songs in your own name. Our participation is to provide you with great, commercial, "royalty-free" music. Since we are not dictating a melody or participating in writing the lyric, the song is all yours! Each track is numbered to correspond with the appropriate chord chart. On each chord chart you will find the key, the tempo, the "roadmap" (the section by section breakdown of the track), and the feel.

The feel is very important in that it will help dictate the length of the "syllables" of melody or lyric. Here are two examples of feel.

Straight 8th feel: Twinkle twinkle little star
How I wonder what you are…..

Each pulse of the lyric and melody has an even duration

Triplet feel: Jack and Jill went up the hill
To fetch a pail of wa-ter

The pulses are in groups of three. In this case, and very commonly, it is broken into a word or note with two pulses, followed by a word with one pulse. In this case "Jack" has two pulses, "and" has one pulse, "Jill" has two pulses, "went" has one, etc. Very simply, every other word has a short duration. The style of the music will dictate this "feel" for your writing.

The next short lecture is on the most important word for you to be aware of as your write, and that word is "symmetry." To me, symmetry encompasses many facets of writing, including your rhyme scheme, your number of syllables per line, even your style of sentence structure. In songwriting, symmetry simply means similar. For example, if the first verse of a song is four lines of eight syllables, the second verse should be very similar to that. Symmetry means that you create an expectation in the person who hears your song that things will be a certain way. The details are up to you and your creative mind, but remember this. When most of us hear a great song for the first time, we find that we can usually sing or hum along by the second "chorus." That is because the symmetry of the writing makes us feel that we are hearing "familiar" material as the song progresses. Whether you are listening to Hank Williams or Babyface, you will hear great symmetry in the writing. You can even change the symmetry later in the song to catch the listener by surprise and get their attention for something you want to say. Become aware of what great writers are doing, and it will make you a better writer.

Next is a brief explanation of song sections. There are no rules that force us to write in pre-determined blocks, but the common song-form uses them, and that is what our ears are used to hearing, so it sounds more like a song to us. The three most important sections are the "verse," the "chorus," and the "bridge." Generally speaking, the "chorus" is a repeated section that contains the "hook" or title lines of the song. The verse is usually the first statement of the story of the song, and generally is used once. A second verse would normally contain the same symmetry as the first verse, but with different lyrics. A bridge, or as we sometimes refer to it, an "escape," is meant to introduce totally new melody, chordal, and lyric substance, and serves to create a little break in the symmetry before we return to a familiar verse or chorus. Each track in this series will also have an instrumental intro and "outro." Some of the tracks will have a brief instrumental solo or "turnaround," which will musically set up the next section, i.e. give you a chance to get a big breath before your next lyric section.

So finally, here are the rules. Guess what—**THERE ARE NO RULES!!!!** You have this music in your hands, have fun. Some of music's greatest songwriters did not set out to write hit songs. They just felt a need to express themselves. Thank goodness they did. The subject matter is up to you. You can write something funny, serious, sad, or nonsense—it is up to you because when you use this package the way it was intended...

YOU WRITE THE SONGS.

For quick and easy-to-understand directions on how to copyright your songs, visit www.music-law.com/registercopyright.html

Produced by Tim Smith

Recorded at The Groovehouse, Nashville, TN

Bass: Tim Smith
Guitars: Roddy Smith
Keyboards: Bobby Ogdin
Drums: Tommy Wells
Steel Guitar: Joe Wright
Fiddle: Billy Contreras
Narration: Troy Duran

N

New Country Vol 1 demonstration track

Key of E

♩ = 148

COUNTRY ROCK/STRAIGHT 8TH FEEL

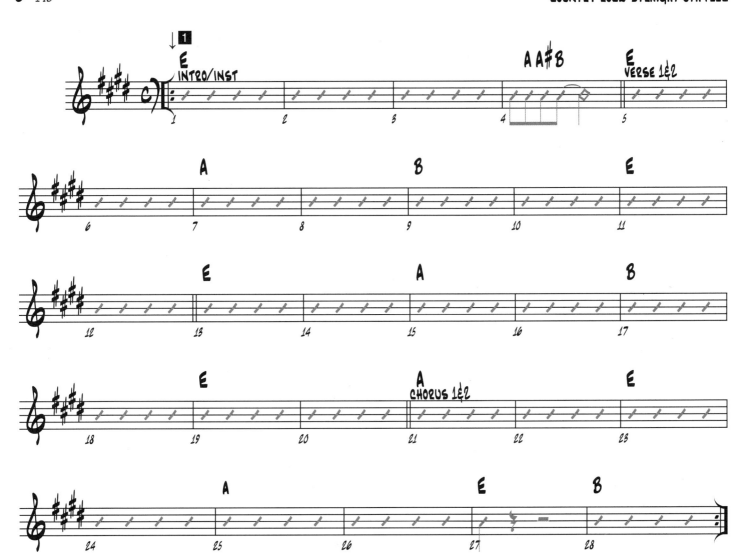

INTRO 4 BARS

VERSE 1 16 BARS

CHORUS 1 8 BARS

INST 4 BARS

VERSE 2 16 BARS

MMO 7021

New Country Vol 1 Track 1

straight 8th feel

Melody and Lyrics by _____

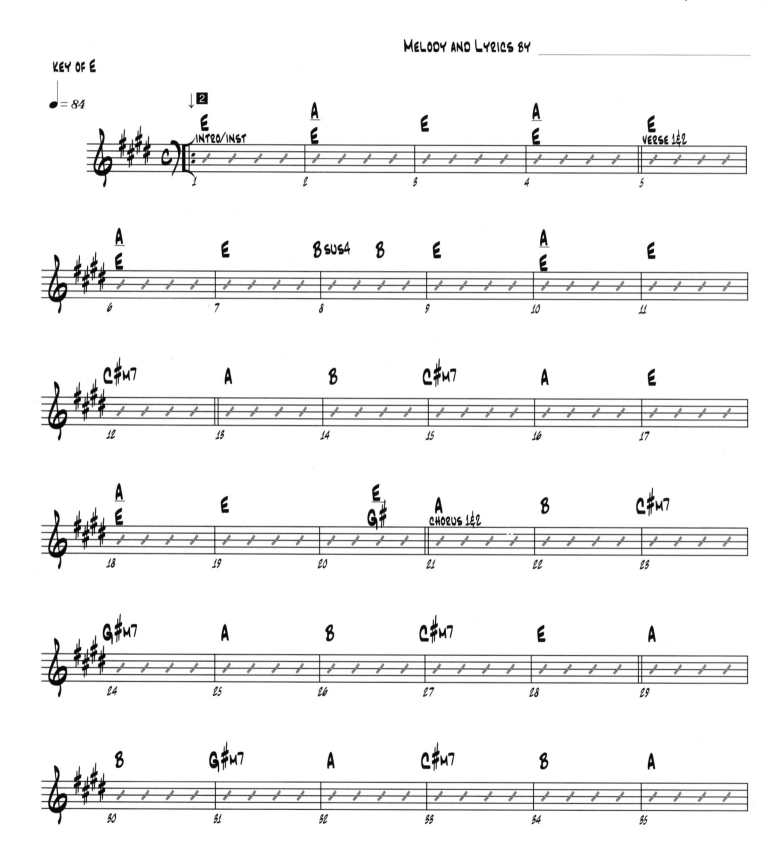

INTRO 4 BARS

VERSE 1 16 BARS

CHORUS 1 16 BARS

INST 4 BARS

VERSE 2 16 BARS

CHORUS 2 16 BARS

BRIDGE 8 BARS

CHORUSES 16 BARS EACH FOR FADE

MMO 7021

New Country Vol 1 Track 2

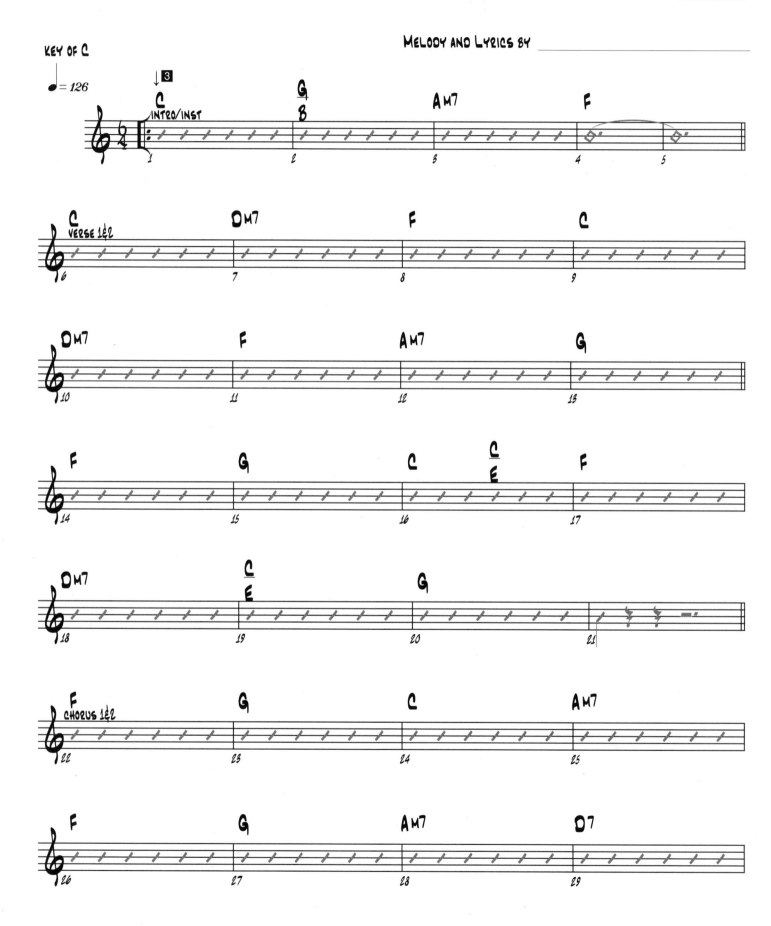

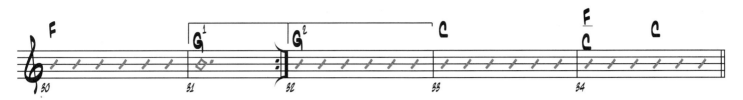

INTRO 5 BARS

VERSE 1 16 BARS

CHORUS 1 10 BARS

INST 5 BARS

VERSE 2 16 BARS

CHORUS 2 10 BARS

TURNAROUND 2 BARS

BRIDGE 8 BARS

CHORUSES 10 BARS

REPEAT TIL FADE

New Country Vol 1 track 3

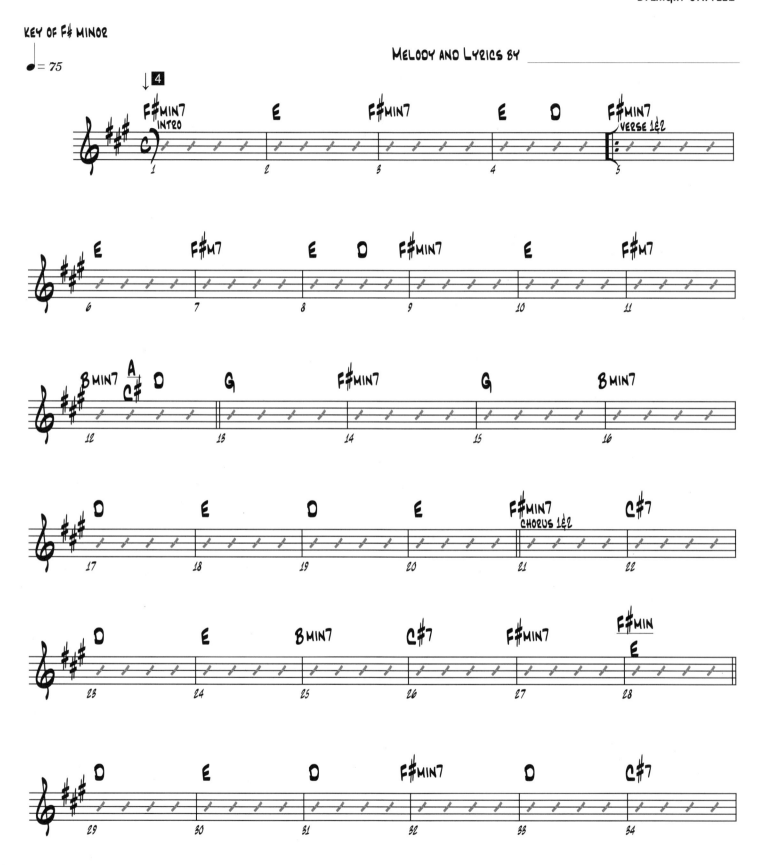

INTRO 4 BARS

VERSE 1 16 BARS

CHORUS 1 16 BARS

VERSE 2 16 BARS

CHORUS 2 16 BARS

INST 8 BARS

CHORUSES 16 BARS

REPEAT TIL FADE

New Country Vol 1 Track 4

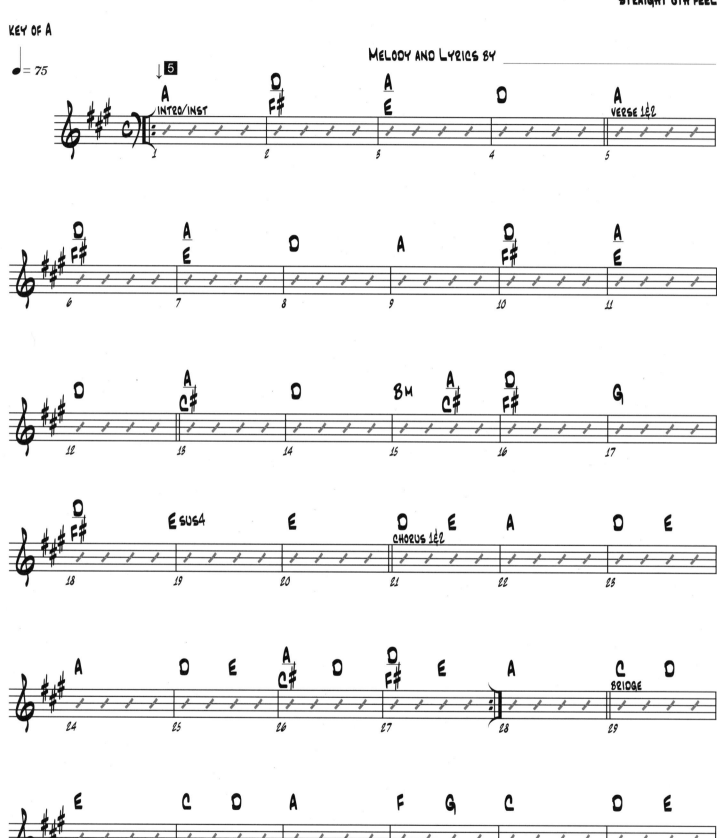

INTRO 4 BARS   INST 4 BARS   BRIDGE 8 BARS   OUTRO 5 BARS
VERSE 1 16 BARS   VERSE 2 16 BARS   CHORUS 3 8 BARS
CHORUS 1 7 BARS   CHORUS 2 8 BARS   TAG 3 BARS

New Country Vol 1 Track 5

STRAIGHT 8TH FEEL

KEY OF C

MELODY AND LYRICS BY _____

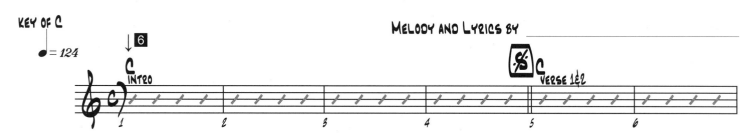

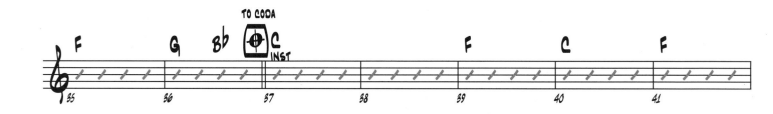

INTRO 4 BARS

VERSE 1 16 BARS

CHORUS 1 16 BARS

INST 16 BARS

VERSE 2 16 BARS

CHORUS 2 16 BARS

CHORUSES 16 BARS

REPEAT TIL FADE

New Country Vol 1 Track 6

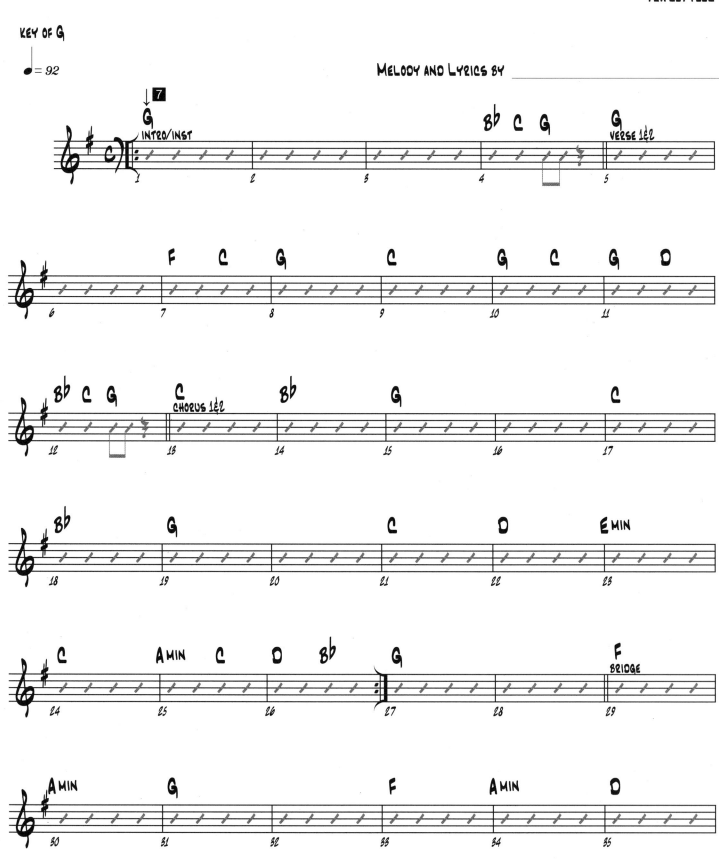

INTRO 4 BARS

VERSE 1 8 BARS

CHORUS 1 14 BARS

INST 1 4 BARS

VERSE 2 8 BARS

CHORUS 2 16 BARS

BRIDGE 8 BARS

INST 2 8 BARS

CHORUS 3 14 BARS

OUTRO 4 BARS

New Country Vol 1 track 7

Triplet feel

INTRO 8 BARS
VERSE 1 16 BARS
VERSE 2 16 BARS
CHORUS 1 16 BARS
INST 8 BARS
VERSE 3 16 BARS
CHORUS 2 16 BARS
CHORUS 3 16 BARS
TAG 6 BARS
OUTRO 7 BARS

New Country Vol 1 Track 8

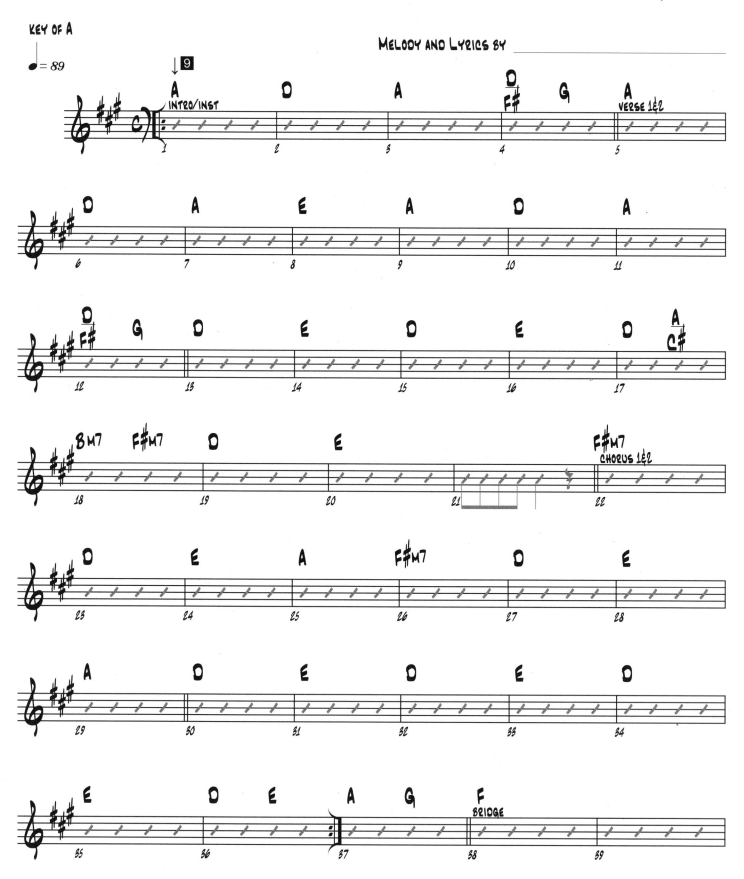

INTRO 4 BARS

VERSE 1 17 BARS

CHORUS 1 15 BARS

INST 4 BARS

VERSE 2 17 BARS

CHORUS 2 16 BARS

BRIDGE 8 BARS

CHORUS 3 15 BARS

CHORUS 4 15 BARS

OUTRO 5 BARS

New Country Vol 1 track 9

straight 8th feel

Melody and Lyrics by _____

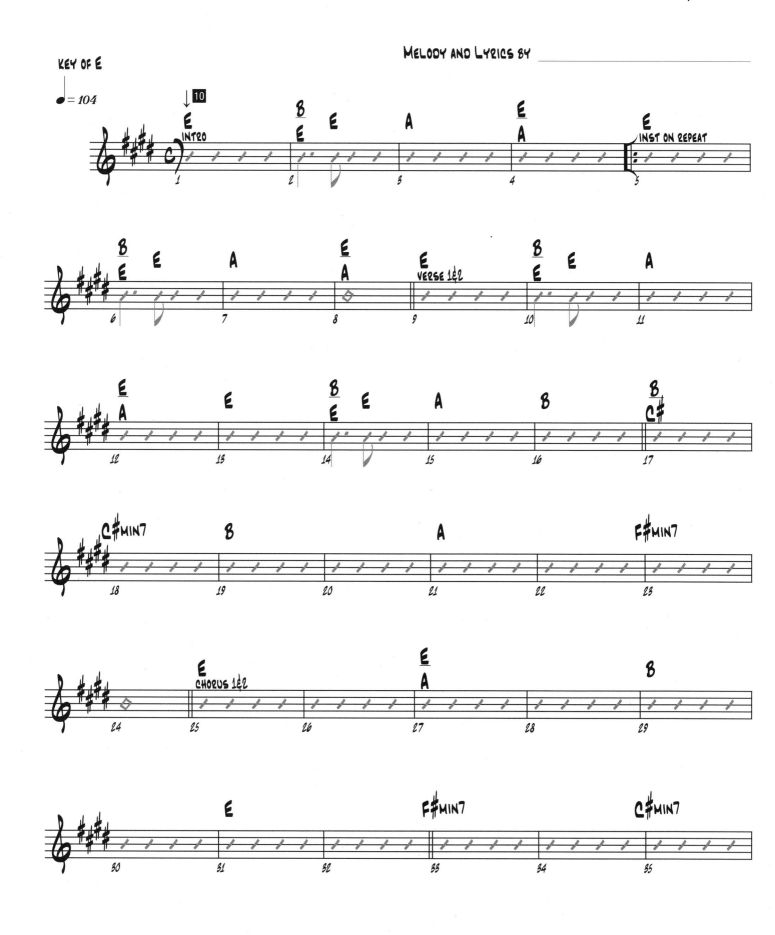

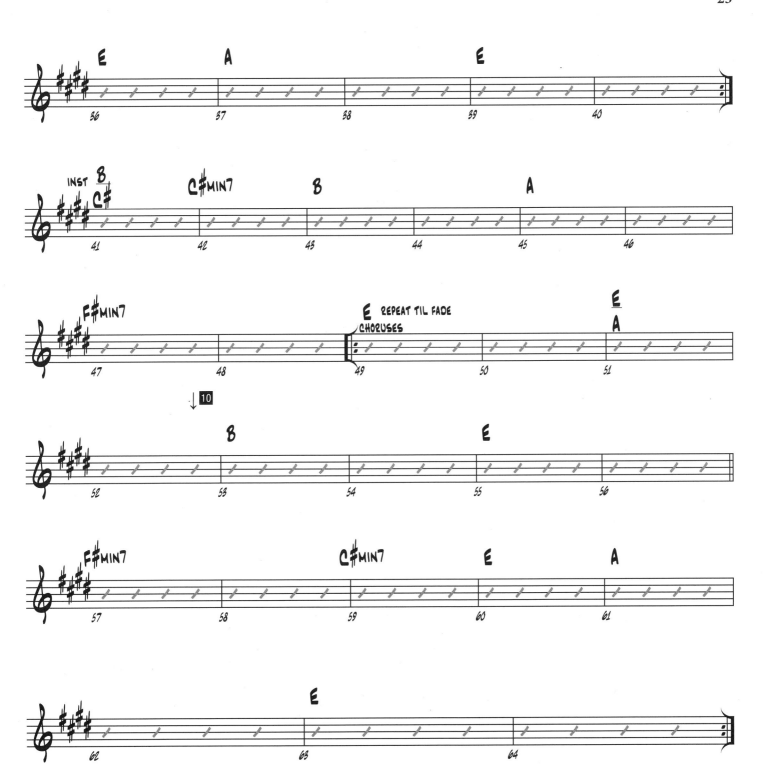

INTRO 8 BARS

VERSE 1 16 BARS

CHORUS 1 16 BARS

INST 4 BARS

VERSE 2 16 BARS

CHORUS 2 16 BARS

INST 2 8 BARS

CHORUSES 16 BARS

REPEAT TIL FADE

MMO 7021

New Country Vol 1 Track 10

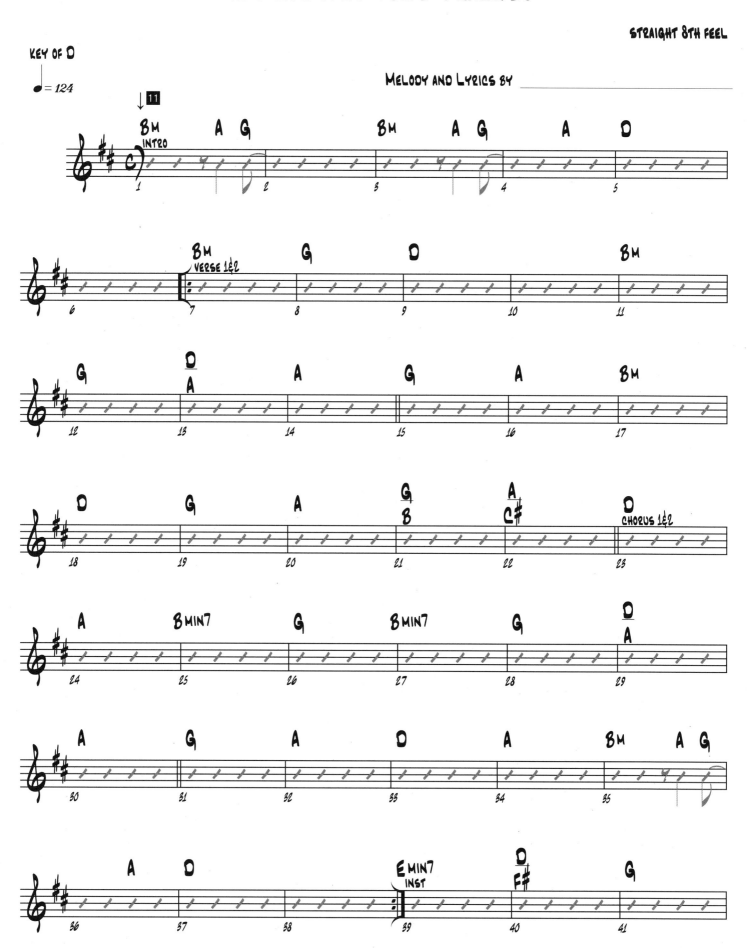

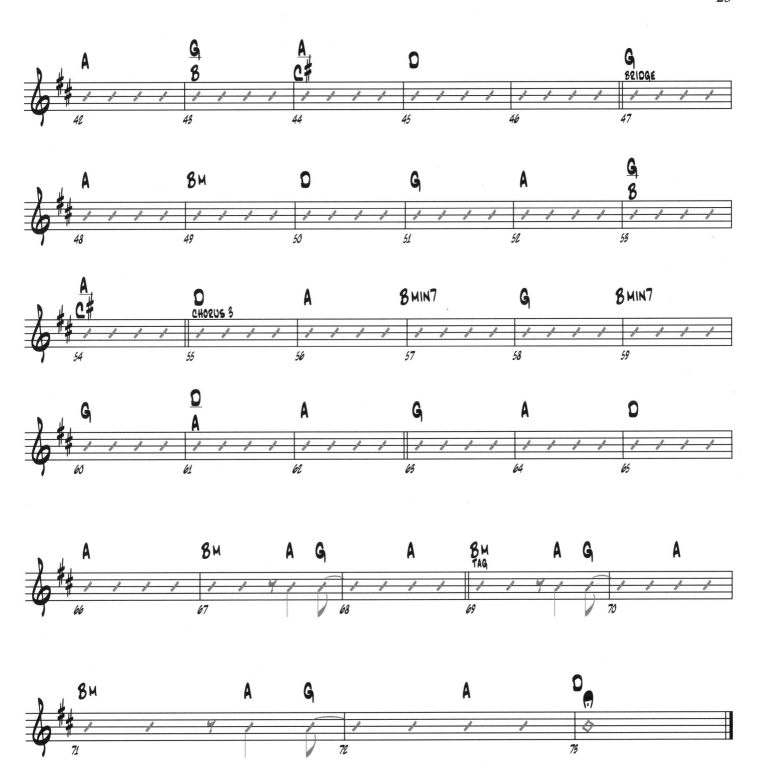

INTRO 6 BARS

VERSE 1 16 BARS

CHORUS 1 16 BARS

VERSE 2 16 BARS

CHORUS 2 16 BARS

INST 8 BARS

BRIDGE 8 BARS

CHORUS 14 BARS

TAG 5 BARS

MELODY AND LYRICS BY _____

MELODY AND LYRICS BY _____

Melody and Lyrics by _____

MELODY AND LYRICS BY _____

MELODY AND LYRICS BY _____

MELODY AND LYRICS BY _____

MUSIC MINUS ONE
50 Executive Boulevard
Elmsford, New York 10523-1325
800-669-7464 (U.S.)/914-592-1188 (International)

www.musicminusone.com
e-mail: info@musicminusone.com

Printed in Canada